SCHOOLS LIBRARY SERVICE

PROJECT STOCK

8372908 3

SUNDERLAND PUBLIC LIBRARIES

This book is due for return to the Library indicated above on or before the last date entered. Fines will be charged at the current rate if the book is kept after that date

lib0160

Conservation

by
JOY PALMER

HODDER AND STOUGHTON
LONDON   SYDNEY   AUCKLAND   TORONTO

Note to the reader
The words in italics are explained in the glossary on page 30

The Author's and Publishers' thanks are due to the following for permission to reproduce photographs:

r = right; l = left; t = top; b = bottom

Heather Angel: 26; Barnaby's Picture Library: 4, 5, 9, 11l, 11r, 12, 13r, 17, 18, 19, 20, 21t, 24; Maggie Murray/Format: 29; Chris Gladwell: 28; Greenpeace Communication Ltd: 23; Oxford Scientific Films: Stuart Bebb/OSF: 15b; Deni Bown/OSF: 7; M. J. Coe/OSF: 13l; Mark Hamblin/OSF: 10, 14; G. A. Maclean/OSF: 15t; Peter O'Toole/OSF: 16b; Richard Packwood/OSF: 21b; Avril Ramage/OSF: 16t; Ronald Toms/OSF: 22; John Poole/RSNC UK2000: cover; G. K. Ward: 25, 27

Artist: John Lobban
Designed by Andrew Shoolbred
Bibliography compiled by Peter Bone
Picture research by Angela Anderson

The Author would like to thank the Association of Agriculture for its help and advice.

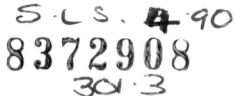

British Library Cataloguing in Publication Data
Palmer, Joy
  Conservation.
    1. Environment. Conservation. — For children
  I. Title   II. Series
  333.7'2
  ISBN 0-340-49925-7

Text copyright © Joy Palmer 1989
Illustrations copyright © John Lobban 1989

First published 1989

All rights reserved. No part of this publication may be reproduced or transmitted in any form or by any means, electronically or mechanically, including photocopying, recording, or any information storage and retrieval system, without either prior permission in writing from the publisher or a licence permitting restricted copying. In the United Kingdom such licences are issued by the Copyright Licensing Agency, 33-34 Alfred Place, London WC1E 7DP.

Published by Hodder and Stoughton Children's Books, a division of Hodder and Stoughton Ltd, Mill Road, Dunton Green, Sevenoaks, Kent TN13 2YA

Photoset by Litho Link Ltd, Welshpool, Powys, Wales

Printed in Belgium by Proost International Book Production

Contents

	page
Introduction	4
Taking care of the natural world	6
Wildlife on a farm	8
Grass as a home	10
Trees as homes	12
Life in hedgerows	14
Water as a home	16
Pests	18
The need for good soil	20
Water pollution	22
Land pollution	24
Taking care of the countryside	26
Further information	28
Glossary	30
Bibliography	31
Index	32

Introduction

The planet Earth is our home, and also the home of countless other animals and plants. All life on Earth depends on its *environment* (surroundings) for its survival. The environment includes land, water, air and sunshine.

▶ The planet Earth is the home of countless animals and plants. The land, water and air must be kept clean for life to survive.

Food chains

The environment provides food for all living things. Plants use air and light from the sun, and water and goodness from the soil to make the foods they need. These foods are called carbohydrates and proteins. They are produced in the green leaves of plants.

Animals cannot make their own food in the same way. They must eat plants or other animals. Some animals eat only plants; many eat other animals (usually smaller than themselves); and some feed on both plants and animals. This linking of plants and animals is called a food chain.

Life and death

The lives of all plants and animals eventually come to an end. The remains of dead plants and animals rot into the ground and mix with the soil, making it richer. In turn, this rich soil helps new plant life grow. This process of death leading to new life is called a natural cycle.

Natural balance

The natural world constantly changes, although there is always a pattern to the changes. When one life ends, another begins; when one season finishes, another starts. Sometimes, this pattern (balance) is upset by a natural event, such as a hurricane, earthquake, tidal wave or drought. Some forms of life are damaged by these events, but in time the natural balance is restored.

▶ The environment provides food for all living things.

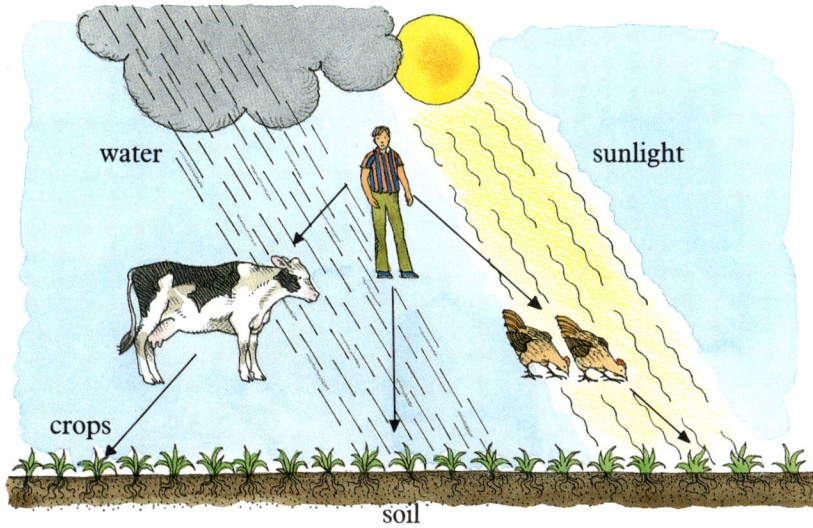

Much of our countryside is very beautiful. Farmers have to think carefully about how best to use their land. ▼

Taking care of the natural world

Human life is part of the natural world, just like any other form of life. We are a link in many food chains and part of the natural cycle. Yet in some ways people are different from other living things. We can think and plan our lives. We can make decisions that may affect plants, animals and our surroundings. For example, building towns and roads means covering large areas of soil. Removing trees and hedgerows alters the countryside and destroys animals' homes. The goodness of the soil can be ruined if chemicals are not used sensibly. Dumping waste can *pollute* supplies of fresh water. Rubbish left in the countryside can harm, or kill animals.

▶ This is a food chain. If one animal or plant is destroyed, the chain is broken and the other animals suffer.

tree bark   woodlouse   small bird   predatory bird

Being responsible

People should think carefully about whether their activities will harm or improve the natural world. A bad decision may destroy some form of life, or harm part of the world forever. For example, if too many trees are cut down there may not be enough seeds or nuts to keep alive the animals who depend on them. If these animals die, all members of a food chain are affected.

    Harming the Earth eventually harms humans too. There is only a thin layer of soil covering the Earth which can be used for farming. There is a limited supply of water and fresh air. If these are damaged then all life on our planet may be threatened.

Conservation

Conservation is all about understanding the *environment* and managing it sensibly. It also means understanding that humans are only a small part of the world and that we depend on many other things for survival. It is up to us to behave in a responsible way towards our world.

▶ All living things are part of the natural cycle of life and death. Decayed matter helps form soil which is food for new life.

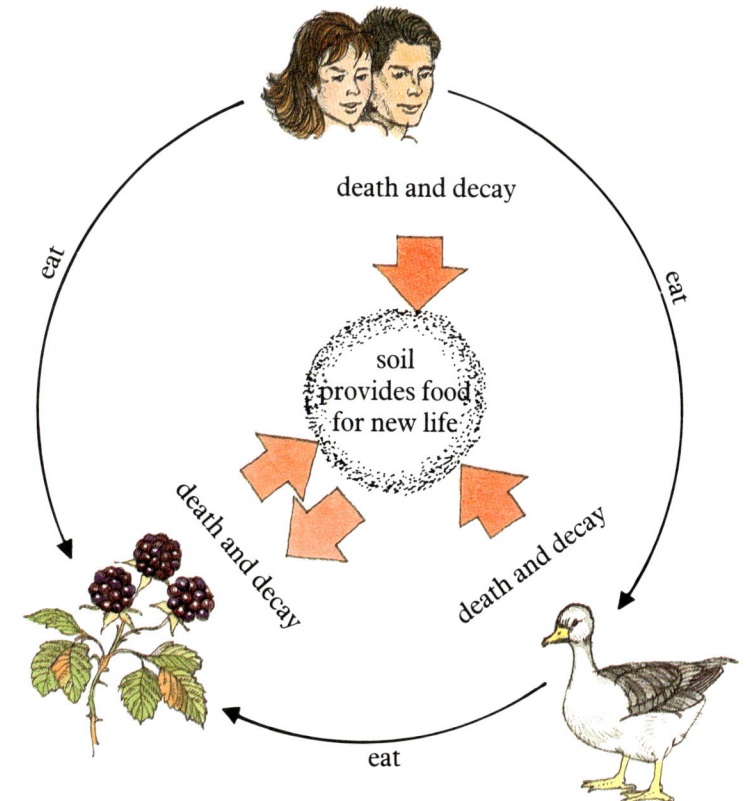

▶ Plants turn their leaves towards the sunshine to absorb as much light as possible.

Wildlife on a farm

A farm is a place for growing *crops* (food plants) and taking care of animals that will provide food. Farmers choose the plants and animals they wish to keep, but other wild animals, including birds and insects, make the farm their home too. There are also wild plants and trees in and around fields and hedgerows. A farm can be a wonderful *nature reserve*, providing a home for a great variety of wildlife.

Animal habitats

If wild animals are to live on a farm or visit it regularly, there must be suitable places for them to eat, sleep, breed and shelter. A suitable home is called a *habitat*. Farms have many good wildlife habitats, such as fields, trees, hedgerows, ponds and streams. Here there are lots of tiny places where wild creatures can live, for example among the stems of grass or under the loose bark of a tree.

▶ Farmland provides countless habitats for wildlife.

▲ Trees and hedgerows are often cut down to make fields bigger. Huge machines, like this harvester, can then work the large fields.

Not all animals like to live in the same kind of place. Some creatures love dark, damp hiding places. Woodlice, for example, crawl underneath loose bark or fallen branches on the ground. Other animals prefer a lighter place, or one underwater.

Unfortunately, a large number of habitats are being destroyed. It is thought that if all the hedgerows which have been cut down were put in a line, they would stretch half-way to the moon! Removing hedges and trees not only makes the countryside look less beautiful, but also robs wild creatures and plants of shelter and food. It also means animals have fewer places to breed, so some species of wildlife may be reduced in number or even disappear altogether in the future.

On the other hand, farming can help animals, and *conservation* in general.

Farmers can create habitats by using their land carefully. For example, every tree and hedgerow they plant increases the number of homes for animals. Much thought should go into planning, or 'managing', any changes to the landscape. Most farmers know that managing their land carefully is a very important part of their job.

Grass as a home

The grassy fields of a farm make an ideal *habitat*. The grass provides food for many small creatures, as well as for sheep and cows. Other animals, such as moles and mice, like to shelter in long grass. These animals attract cats, foxes and weasels hunting for food. Together they form one of the farm's natural food chains.

Grass roots provide a home for much smaller creatures, such as worms, spiders and insects. These are hunted by birds, such as starlings and blackbirds. Other birds visit grassy fields for a different sort of food. Finches, for example, come to collect and eat the seeds found in long grass.

▶ Birds such as finches visit grassy fields to find seeds and insects to eat.

A flower meadow

If a farmer does not cut or mow a field, it may become a *meadow* with long grass and flowers. This is even more attractive to wildlife. The brightly coloured flowers attract bees and wasps in search of nectar for food. As the insects fly from one flower to another, they carry tiny grains of pollen on the hairs on their bodies. Some pollen grains are brushed off and left behind in the flowers. In this way, an important process called *pollination* can begin. Pollination has to take place before a flower can produce the seeds which will grow into new plants.

Meadow flowers also attract beautiful butterflies which lay eggs and produce caterpillars. These caterpillars form an important part of a meadow's food chain because birds and small mammals often come in search of them for food.

The many different flowers are an important part of life on a farm. In spring, they may include daisies, cowslips, cuckoo flowers and wild daffodils. Later in the year speedwells, yellow rattle, yarrow and harebells may grow.

Some meadow plants, however, are becoming rare. There are two possible reasons for this. First, there are fewer meadows nowadays. Second, many of those that do remain are mown regularly. This means that flowers and seeds are unable to grow and produce new plants. So if a meadow is to aid *conservation*, farmers must plan their work very carefully. Many farmers do just this, and some have even won special prizes and awards for their efforts.

▲ Wild flowers attract insects.

▲ Buttercups are common meadow plants.

Trees as homes

Trees provide homes for many different animals. Birds and insects find shelter amongst the branches and leaves, and in the bark of the trunk. Blue tits, great tits, robins, wrens, blackbirds and thrushes nest in the branches, while beetles, spiders and woodlice tunnel through cracks and crevices in the bark.

Trees not only provide shelter; they are also a good source of food. Some creatures, such as caterpillars, eat the leaves. Others prefer the flowers. Many come in search of fruits, nuts and seeds.

The ground under a tree, or group of trees, also attracts a variety of animals. There may be dead, rotting leaves, old branches, and fruits and seeds. Animals such as mice, hedgehogs, foxes, weasels and squirrels come to find food and shelter. Birds peck at the ground for food. Tiny creatures such as spiders, beetles, millipedes, centipedes, worms and woodlice burrow into the dead leaves and rotting bark, in search of a dark, damp place in which to shelter.

Grey squirrels are commonly found in wooded areas on farms. ▼

▶ Mosses and lichens both live on the bark of trees.

Woodlice tunnel into tree bark to make their homes. ▼

A home for plants
Trees also attract plant life. Mosses and lichens both live on the bark of trees. This is why some tree trunks are bright green. Beautiful flowers, such as primroses and bluebells, live in the shelter of trees, as do other non-flowering plants such as ferns, mushrooms and toadstools.

Cutting down trees
Trees are important on a farm. First, they form a natural barrier which provides shelter from wind and rain. Second, their roots 'grip' the soil and help to stop it being washed away by wind and rain. Unfortunately, farmers sometimes need to cut down trees to get more space for their animals and machinery, or because the trees are diseased. As a result, there are now fewer trees in the countryside than there were a hundred years ago. This is something we should be worried about. Not only are trees beautiful to look at, but they provide food and shelter for a variety of animals and plants.

Fortunately, some farmers realise this and are helping to *conserve* trees on their farmland. Young trees, called saplings, are being planted, for example oaks and birches.

Life in hedgerows

When small trees and shrubs are planted in a line to make a thick barrier, the barrier is called a hedge, or hedgerow. Thousands of kilometres of hedgerows have been planted by farmers during the last three or four hundred years. Holly, hazel, hawthorn, dogwood, blackthorn and guelder rose are all plants which make good hedgerows. These are used because they do not grow too tall. Indeed, if they are trimmed regularly at the top, they grow wider at the bottom, making a good thick hedge. Taking care of these hedges is an important part of a farmer's work.

Hedges are important to farmers because they provide shelter for farm animals such as sheep and cows. The animals lie against a hedge to protect themselves from wind, rain, or snow. Without hedgerows, some animals would certainly die in very cold weather.

▶ Hedgerows provide plenty of shelter for birds' nests.

A home for wildlife

Hedges are also important because they attract a large number of wild creatures and plants. Hedgehogs, mice, weasels, voles and rabbits find a safe home here, sheltered by the twigs and leaves overhead. Birds and insects nest, breed and find food in the shape of seeds, berries, flowers, roots and leaves. Grasses and wild flowers grow beneath the hedge, and so provide more shelter amongst the roots and thin trunks of the trees.

▶ Elder and dogrose are flowering plants commonly found in hedgerows.

Many different food chains exist in a hedge. For example caterpillars which live and feed on the leaves are hunted by larger animals such as thrushes and other small birds. In turn, these will be eaten by even larger animals such as weasels or sparrow-hawks. Mice and insects will be hunted by other enemies such as owls.

Unfortunately, hedges are also a disappearing *habitat*. As with trees, some farmers have removed hedgerows in order to make larger open fields suited to modern machinery. They also want to save the time and money needed to take good care of the hedgerows. This may seem good sense to the farmer, but it is in fact very short-sighted. Once a hedgerow is lost, then so too is the wildlife which relied upon it for food and shelter.

▶ Hedgerows need constant care to keep them healthy. This one is being trimmed so it will grow thicker.

Water as a home

Life cannot exist without water. Animals and plants all need a regular supply to stay alive. Many farmers have water on their land, perhaps in the form of a pond or stream, which attracts both farm animals and wildlife in the area. Even a large puddle may attract visitors to drink.

At home in a pond

A pond in the countryside is likely to contain a wide variety of tiny creatures. These may include pond snails, pond skaters, water boatmen, beetles, dragonflies and damselflies. There may also be amphibians – larger animals with backbones such as frogs, newts and toads, which spend part of their lives in water and part on land. Some creatures make the pond their permanent home. Many others, such as birds, bats, hedgehogs and mice visit the pond to drink or bathe. A pond is always a lively and exciting place, so long as the water stays fresh and clean.

▶ Frogs are attracted to farm ponds, so long as the water is clean and fresh.

▶ Pond skaters are tiny insects which walk across the surface of ponds.

▲ A wide variety of wild plants live near farmland ponds.

Many wild flowers and plants like to live near water: others grow best when their roots are actually in the water. A pond or stream may therefore support a wide range of plant life. Some wild flowers to be found at the edge of water include the flag iris, marsh marigold, meadow sweet and ragged robin. As well as being lovely to look at, these flowers provide food, shelter and nesting places for birds, amphibians and other small animals.

Unfortunately, ponds share the same problem as trees and hedgerows. Many have been removed to create bigger fields and leave more room for large modern farm machinery. Because of this, some inhabitants of ponds, such as the Great Crested Newt, are becoming very rare. Indeed, it is quite possible that certain forms of waterlife may soon disappear altogether.

Fortunately, some farmers are making new ponds. These quickly attract many new forms of wildlife. Even so, ponds, like trees and hedgerows, must be looked after. This is the job of the farmer who has made them.

Pests

More and more people agree that animal and plant life should be protected. But does this mean protecting *all* forms of wildlife? Some animals hinder the work of the farmer. For example, foxes kill chickens and ducks for food. Wild birds often steal seeds and feed on *crops*. Slugs, snails and caterpillars eat their way through fruits and vegetables. As a result, all these animals are given the name of pests.

If pests are not controlled, the amount of food a farmer can raise is reduced.

Pest control

Controlling pests is a problem. By far the easiest way is to kill them by spraying crops with chemicals called *pesticides*. These include insecticides, which kill insects in particular. Many farmers use this method.

Foxes are often regarded as pests by farmers because they kill chickens and ducks for food. ▼

▶ Insect pests are killed by spraying the fields with chemicals called insecticides.

Unfortunately, pesticides do not only kill pests, but also many harmless insects, birds and animals. Food chains are affected. For example, an owl may take in pesticides by eating another bird which has eaten seeds that have been sprayed by chemicals.

Pesticides cause further harm by being washed off plants and soil by the rain. They are carried to streams and rivers, where they may kill fish and other forms of water life. All chemicals may upset the balance of nature, and should be used very carefully – if at all.

Pesticides contain chemicals which can be harmful if they are washed off the land, carried down rivers and into the sea. ▼

19

The need for good soil

Soil is essential for food production. Without it there would be no cereals, fruits or vegetables. Nor would there be any animals since they need grass and other plants which grow in the soil.

If a farmer is to grow healthy *crops*, there must be plenty of goodness in the soil to give the plants the food that they need. When fields are used over and over again for raising crops, the goodness in the soil may be used up. Eventually the soil may become *infertile*, with the result that new plants will not grow.

Fertilisers and weedkillers

Farmers use artificial *fertilisers* to help put goodness back into the soil, and enable more crops to grow. Some people believe that eating crops which have been treated with artificial fertilisers is harmful. They would prefer a more natural fertiliser to be used, such as the manure from animals. However, on a large farm spreading manure is a long job, and many farmers find it easier to use artificial treatments.

A harvest can be increased if the farmer makes sure there are no weeds in the fields. Weeds are plants growing in the wrong place; even beautiful wild flowers may be considered weeds if they are found among food plants. Weeds are harmful because they use the light, water and soil needed by the crops. As a result, the crops grow more slowly and are more thinly spread. To avoid this happening, farmers often spray chemicals on to the fields. These kill the weeds but do not damage the main crop.

▶ This muck-spreader is throwing manure on to the field to make the soil more fertile.

▶ Rich fertile soil is necessary for healthy crops to grow.

Problems
Chemical weedkillers are a problem because they kill plants which some animals feed on. For example, if wild flowers, seeds and berries disappear, then a variety of birds, bees and butterflies lose a valuable source of food. They will have to find food elsewhere, or starve.

Fortunately, some farmers are becoming concerned about the effects of chemical weedkillers and are using them more carefully. Flowers such as poppies and cornflowers are becoming common again. Their red and blue petals are not only beautiful to look at, but attract a wide variety of insects.

▶ Wild flowers are considered weeds if they grow among food plants. They use the light, soil and water needed by the crops.

Water pollution

If any part of the natural world is made dirty or impure, it is said to be polluted. *Pollution* is a serious problem on farms and in the countryside, affecting the land and its water supplies.

Water can become polluted very easily. Artificial *fertilisers*, weedkillers and insecticides are washed out of the soil by rain, then carried into streams and rivers, and eventually into the sea. Throughout their long journey, these

small fish   larger fish, such as cod   humans

▲ If water becomes polluted, the harmful chemicals affect all the animals in the food chain.

▶ These trout have been killed by pollution from a nearby farm.

chemicals may harm or kill water life. If fish containing the remains of chemicals are eaten by birds, the birds are also affected. In this way, food chains help to pass on the damaging effects of pollution.

Many rivers in Britain now have far fewer fish than they did twenty years ago. Indeed, some streams and rivers have no wildlife at all because they are so full of chemicals. Not all these chemicals come from farms. Factories, too, sometimes discharge them into nearby rivers. Fortunately, there are now laws in Britain to stop this happening.

The need for conservation

Preventing water pollution in the countryside is an important part of nature *conservation*. Clean water is essential for healthy plants, animals and humans alike.

If streams and rivers are allowed to become badly polluted, the chemicals will be washed out to the sea. More and more fish will be poisoned. People who depend on fishing for their livelihood will have no work as there will be fewer fish to catch. More importantly, a valuable source of food will have been destroyed.

This sign has been put up to protest against waste being poured into the sea. ▼

Land pollution

Wherever people live, there is bound to be rubbish. Every day, people fill bins and sacks, boxes and bags with leftover food scraps, packages and cartons, old clothes, broken objects and other things which are no longer needed. Most of this household waste goes into dustbins which are emptied regularly. The rubbish is taken to places where it can be burnt or buried underground.

Unfortunately, some people are careless with their rubbish. They may take it into the countryside and throw it away, perhaps at the edge of a field, under a hedgerow or into a stream. Large items like old mattresses, broken TV sets, and washing machines are often dumped in this way. Old cans, picnic wrappings and bottles are often thrown away by passers-by who do not stop to think of the problems they may cause.

Dumped litter not only looks ugly, but can harm or even kill wildlife. ▼

▲ How do you think this litter can harm wildlife?

Rubbish and litter spoil the beauty of the countryside, making it untidy, unsafe and unclean. Some rubbish is actually dangerous. Animals may tread on broken glass and cut themselves. They may also eat items such as plastic bags and ring pulls from old cans, both of which can cause death. Many farmers can tell sad stories of animals which have been injured or died in accidents involving rubbish.

Injuries and deaths like these can be avoided. In fact, much of our household rubbish can be put to good use. Paper, rags, old cans, glass bottles, plastic containers and pieces of metal can all be collected, processed and used again. This is called *recycling*. Nowadays many council rubbish dumps have special containers for different types of rubbish so that more can be recycled.

▶ Much rubbish can be put to good use. For example, glass bottles can be collected, processed and used again.

25

Taking care of the countryside

In 1981 Parliament passed a law called The Wildlife and Countryside Act to help protect birds, animals and plants, especially those which are becoming rare. It is now against the law to remove eggs from the nests of wild birds, or to move certain animals such as Great Crested Newts, which are known as protected species. It is also illegal to pick the flowers of protected plants or to collect their seeds. Anyone who is caught breaking these laws receives a heavy fine.

▶ Kingfishers are just one species now protected by The Wildlife and Countryside Act of 1981.

Keep the Country Code

The Country Code is a set of rules advising people how to behave sensibly in the countryside. The Code helps to keep people safe, and to protect farmlife and wildlife. It should always be obeyed when visiting farms and country areas. You will find it on page 28.

▶ Picking up litter is one way we can help protect the countryside.

Keep caring about conservation

We must always remember that our own lives depend on good soil and the plants which grow there. We also need clean, fresh water and air. Indeed, all living things depend on each other for survival. To care about all forms of life and the earth which supports them is to care about the balance of nature. Human life is part of this delicate balance. To upset this balance means doing harm to all living things, including ourselves.

It is wrong to disturb any animals or plants, even those which are not specifically protected by law. All living things should be taken care of. They are all essential for maintaining the natural balance. They are also beautiful and make our world an attractive place.

27

Further information

When you are out in the countryside, always keep the rules of the Country Code. These are:

1. Enjoy the countryside and respect its life and worth.
2. Guard against all risk of fire.
3. Fasten all gates.
4. Keep your dogs under close control.
5. Keep to public paths across farmland.
6. Use gates and stiles to cross fences, hedges and walls.
7. Leave livestock, crops and machinery alone.
8. Take your litter home.
9. Help to keep all water clean.
10. Protect wildlife, plants and trees.
11. Take special care on country roads.
12. Make no unnecessary noise.

▶ It is important to keep towns and cities clean too. Any dirty environment is unpleasant and unhealthy.

Useful addresses

The organisations listed below will provide more information about conservation if you write to them, enclosing a stamped, addressed envelope.

The Association of Agriculture, Victoria Chambers, 16-20 Strutton Ground, London SW1P 2HP

Information Department, Friends of the Earth Ltd, 26-28 Underwood Street, London N1 7JQ

The NFU Farming Information Centre, Agriculture House, Knightsbridge, London SW1X 7NJ

Information and Library Service, Nature Conservancy Council, Northminster House, Peterborough PE1 1VA

WATCH, 22 The Green, Nettleham, Lincoln LN2 2NR

▶ People are becoming more aware of the need to care for the countryside. This protest is against the Channel Tunnel railway line being laid across farmland.

Glossary

Conservation Taking care of the environment and life on earth.

Crops Food plants, grown by a farmer.

Environment Surroundings.

Fertiliser Something which helps to make soil richer and better for growing plants.

Habitat The natural home of animals and plants.

Infertile soil Soil that does not have enough natural goodness left to enable new plants to grow.

Meadow A field of grass that is not cut or disturbed.

Nature reserve Land which provides homes for wild creatures and plants.

Pesticide A chemical for killing plant pests such as insects.

Pollination The transfer of pollen from one flower to another, usually by insects.

Pollution Making any part of the natural world dirty or impure. Water, land and air may all be polluted.

Recycling The re-use of waste materials, turning them into something that is useful.

Bibliography

If you want to find out more about conservation the following books may be of interest. Your local library should be able to get copies for you.

Bright, Michael.
POLLUTION AND WILDLIFE.
Franklin Watts, 1987.   0863135420

Of particular interest are the sections on pesticides and insecticides, and how they affect the food chain.

Gilman, David.
THE WILDLIFE OF FARMLAND.
Macdonald, 1983.   0356071251

Helpful background information on the farm as a wildlife habitat.

Books for older children and adults

Bowman, Keith.
AGRICULTURE.
Macdonald Educational, 1985.   0356071170

A general book on farming which has a good section on how farming can lead to changes in the environment. There is a good explanation of soil erosion.

Golland, Derrick.
PRESSURES ON THE COUNTRYSIDE.
Dryad Press, 1986.   0852196253

A general look at the conservation of the countryside, and how many aspects of modern life threaten rural Britain.

Lean, Mary.
POLLUTION AND THE ENVIRONMENT.
Macdonald, 1988.   035610141X

Has a good section which debates the theory that pollution is beginning to affect the climate and, therefore eventually it will affect farmers. A section also looks at the "nitrate time bomb".

Peter Bone
Senior Librarian
Children's and Schools Services, Hampshire County Library

Index

air 4, 6, 27
amphibians 16, 17
animals 4, 6, 8, 9, 10, 12, 13, 14, 15, 16, 17, 18, 19, 20, 21, 22, 23, 25, 26, 27, 28

balance of nature 5, 19, 27
birds 8, 10, 12, 14, 15, 16, 17, 18, 19, 21, 23, 26

chemicals 6, 18, 19, 20, 21, 22, 23
conservation 6, 9, 11, 13, 23, 27, 30
Country Code 26, 28
crops 8, 18, 20, 21, 28, 30

fertilisers 20, 22, 30
food chains 4, 6, 10, 11, 15, 19, 22, 23

grass 10-11, 14, 20

habitats 8, 9, 10, 15, 30
hedgerows 6, 8, 9, 14, 15, 17, 24, 28

infertile soil 20, 30
insects 8, 9, 10, 11, 12, 13, 14, 15, 16, 18, 19, 21

litter 6, 24, 25, 27, 28

meadow 10, 11, 30

natural cycle 4, 6, 7
nature reserve 8, 30

pesticides 18, 19, 22, 30
pests 18-19
plants 4, 6, 7, 8, 10, 11, 13, 14, 15, 16, 17, 18, 19, 20, 21, 26, 27, 28
pollination 10, 30
pollution 6, 22, 23, 24-25, 30
ponds 8, 16, 17

recycling 25, 30

soil 4, 6, 7, 13, 19, 20, 21, 22, 27
sunshine 4, 7, 20, 21

The Wildlife and Countryside Act 26
trees 6, 8, 9, 12, 13, 14, 15, 17, 28

water 4, 6, 8, 16, 17, 19, 20, 21, 22, 23, 27, 28
weedkillers 20-21, 22
weeds 20-21